CIVIL WAR
HIGHLIGHTS

HOME FRONT
1861–1865

TIM COOKE

A⁺

Smart Apple Media

This edition published in 2013 by

Smart Apple Media, an imprint of Black Rabbit Books

PO Box 3263, Mankato, MN 56002

www.blackrabbitbooks.com

Brown Bear Books Ltd.

Editorial Director: Lindsey Lowe
Managing Editor: Tim Cooke
Children's Publisher: Anne O'Daly
Picture Manager: Sophie Mortimer
Creative Director: Jeni Child

Library of Congress Cataloging-in-Publication Data
Cooke, Tim, 1961-
  Home front, 1861-1865 / edited by Tim Cooke.
     p. cm. -- (Civil War highlights)
  Includes bibliographical references and index.
  Summary: "In an alphabetical almanac format, describes life on
the home front during the US Civil War. Explains how daily life
was affected differently in the North than in the South, and
describes the sacrifices people made toward the war efforts.
Includes a timeline and study features to help readers focus on
important information"--Provided by publisher.
  ISBN 978-1-59920-817-6 (library binding)
  1. United States--History--Civil War, 1861-1865--Social aspects-
-Juvenile literature. 2. Confederate States of America--Social
conditions--Juvenile literature. I. Title.
  E468.9.C66 2013
  973.7'1--dc23
                                     2012001307

Printed in the United States of America at Corporate
Graphics, North Mankato, Minnesota

PO1437
2-2012

9 8 7 6 5 4 3 2 1

Contents

Introduction

For those not caught up in the fighting, life during the Civil War varied greatly. For some people in the North, life carried on largely as normal; in the South, the war impacted every aspect of life.

For many people in the South, the war was an immediate experience. Most of the fighting took place on Southern territory. Southern cities came under direct attack. A larger proportion of men were in the army, so Southern women had to run farms and plantations, as well as looking after families and households. As the war went on, the Union blockade halted overseas trade. The Southern economy was devastated. All sorts of commodities were in short supply, from agricultural tools to basic foods. Life was a struggle to survive.

In the North, some people made huge profits by selling military equipment and supplies. Among the working poor of the great Northern cities, however, wartime conditions

This kitchen from just after the war includes a range in the center, which was used for cooking as well as heating water.

In this illustration from 1866, a wounded soldier arrives home. Family life was greatly affected by the war.

worsened the tensions that already existed between different ethnic groups.

And in both the North and the South, the war had a great effect on families. Many thousands of husbands, fathers, and sons went to war; and thousands of them were killed or wounded. In the South, in particular, there were few families that did not lose at least one person in the war.

This book

Home Front describes how the conflict changed life for those who stayed at home in both the North and the South: what they ate, what they wore, and how they lived. It also examines some of the most influential individuals of this crucial time. A timeline that runs across the bottom of the pages throughout the book traces the course of the war on the battlefield along with other developments in North America and the rest of the world. At the back of the book is a Need to Know feature, which will help you relate subjects to your school studies.

Buildings and Homes

The influence of mass production was clearly visible in American homes before and after the war. They were often decorated in ornate styles, with dark furniture and rich colors.

This typical house of the period was used as a hospital after the Battle of White Oak Swamp in 1862.

Freed from family farms, people instead worked in towns and cities. A prosperous city dweller in the North might build a two-story masonry house. A less well-off clerk might move his family to the new suburbs. A poor family could only afford to

1861 January–March

CIVIL WAR

JANUARY 2, SOUTH CAROLINA Fort Johnson in Charleston Harbor is occupied by Confederate troops.

JANUARY 5, ALABAMA Alabama troops seize forts Morgan and Gaines, giving Confederate forces control of Mobile Bay.

JANUARY 9, MISSISSIPPI Leaders vote to leave the Union. Mississippi is the second state to join the Confederacy.

JANUARY 10, FLORIDA Florida leaves the Union.

JANUARY 11, ALABAMA Alabama leaves the Union.

OTHER EVENTS

JANUARY 15, UNITED STATES Engineer Elisha Otis invents the safety elevator.

JANUARY 29, UNITED STATES Kansas joins the Union as the 34th state.

January

rent a small apartment in a tenement building shared with other renters. In rural areas of the North, a family might build a farmhouse or occupy an older one.

Likewise, in the Southern states a wealthy merchant in New Orleans might live in a fashionable two-story brick dwelling, although most rural areas of the South had a different architecture. A nonslaveholding farmer might live in a simple wooden frame house.

Usually people used building materials that were easily available nearby. In the forested areas of the Southeast and Northeast, people built wooden frame houses and log cabins. In the Southwest, people built houses of adobe (mud) bricks.

Interior decoration

How a house appeared from the outside was a good indication of a family's status and wealth. In the same way, the look of the rooms inside also gave clues to anyone who visited the home. Before the mid-19th century, one room usually served several purposes: socializing, sleeping, and even eating. Now rooms became specialized. A hall, formal parlor, family parlor, dining room, library, bedroom—all had specific functions and dictated certain activities and behavior. Interior decoration became popular, and magazines and books giving advice on matters such as colors, furniture, lighting, and wallpapers became essential reading for the wealthy.

A tenement building on the Lower East Side, Manhattan, illustrated in Harper's Weekly.

JANUARY 19, GEORGIA
Georgia votes to leave the Union.

JANUARY 26, LOUISIANA
Louisiana becomes the sixth state to leave the Union.

FEBRUARY 4, ALABAMA
Leaders from the South meet in the state capital, Montgomery. They choose Jefferson Davis of Mississippi as their president and write a constitution for the Confederate States of America.

FEBRUARY 7, ALABAMA/MISSISSIPPI
The Choctaw Indian Nation forms an alliance with the South. Other Indian tribes follow later.

FEBRUARY, UNITED STATES
The first moving picture system is patented.

MARCH, RUSSIA
Czar Alexander II abolishes serfdom (a form of slavery).

February   March

Clothing

One of the most visible effects of the Civil War on daily life was in how people dressed. Many men were in uniform. Women in the South faced shortages that limited their choices of clothing.

This drawing depicts an African American family in typical clothes in their cabin in Virginia.

In the years immediately before the war, people wore clothes that were a clear indication of their social class and wealth. There were some common fashions, but there was a huge variety in the style, fabric, and sewing of outfits. For those who

1861
April–June

CIVIL WAR

APRIL 12, SOUTH CAROLINA Confederates fire on Fort Sumter in Charleston Harbor in the first shots of the Civil War.

APRIL 15, THE NORTH President Lincoln calls for 75,000 recruits across the North to fight the South.

APRIL 19, WASHINGTON, D.C. President Lincoln declares a naval blockade of Southern states.

APRIL 19, BALTIMORE Mayor George Brown bans Union troops from the city after they are attacked by an angry pro-Confederate mob.

OTHER EVENTS

APRIL, EGYPT A search party sets out from Cairo to find the explorers John Speke and James Grant, who have gone missing while looking for the source of the Nile River.

April

had to work, both men's and women's clothes were designed to be practical and not to wear out easily. The wealthy, by contrast, wore clothes that were more concerned with fitting the social conventions of the day than with practicality. The fashionable costume of the time was based on the crinoline—a full skirt over a hooped wire frame.

All women wore many layers of clothing, including undergarments, a corset, a dress with a fitted upper part, or bodice, and a cape. Few women of any class would go out without a bonnet to cover their hair, which was considered immodest.

The formal dress of the time can be seen in this postwar photograph of Ulysses S. Grant (seated, center) and his family.

Making clothes

Women of all classes were brought up to sew and knit. While rich families had their clothes made, less well-off women made clothes for themselves and their families. After the invention of Isaac Singer's sewing machine in 1851, the process became quicker, as garments no longer had to be hand stitched.

Children's clothes were designed to last. They were often made with seams that could be let out as the child grew. Until the age of five, boys and girls looked the same, as they both wore petticoats. After the age of five, boys wore pants or knickerbockers (baggy pants gathered below the knee). Girls

APRIL 23, VIRGINIA Major General Robert E. Lee becomes commander of land and naval forces in Virginia.

APRIL 27, WASHINGTON, D.C. Abraham Lincoln suspends "habeus corpus," a law that protects individuals from being arrested for little reason.

MAY 9, GREAT BRITAIN Britain announces it will remain neutral in the Civil War.

MAY 20, NORTH CAROLINA North Carolina is the last state to leave the Union.

JUNE 20, VIRGINIA West Virginia is unhappy at Virginia's decision to leave the Union. It breaks from the Confederacy and is admitted into the Union.

APRIL, AUSTRALIA Robert Burke and William Wills, who led the first expedition across Australia, narrowly miss a rendezvous with their colleagues; Burke and Wills will die in the Outback.

JUNE, UNITED STATES "Aeronaut" Thaddeus Lowe demonstrates his hot-air balloon for President Abraham Lincoln.

May

June

HOMESPUN WOOL AND COTTON

"The Southern Girl with the Homespun Dress" was a popular wartime song. Its lyrics told of the sacrifice made by Southern women: "My homespun dress is plain... But then it shows what Southern girls for Southern rights will do." As new cloth became scarcer, women made their own fabric. This meant homespun wool and cotton. Rich Southerners dusted off their family spinning wheels and looms while poor Southerners, who had always spun their own cloth, found their skills in demand. Homespun was acceptable when used for dresses, but as undergarments and nightwear it was very uncomfortable.

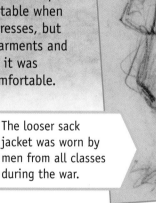

The looser sack jacket was worn by men from all classes during the war.

covered their dresses with aprons or pinafores to keep them clean, because clothes were not washed often. Zippers had not been invented, so all clothing was fastened with buttons.

Like children's clothes, men's clothes did not vary much. Men of all social classes always wore a vest and jacket. During the Civil War, a looser sack coat became a popular replacement for the formal jacket. In the North, New York and Boston were home to a growing garment industry, which mass-produced ready-to-wear suits. The need to produce large numbers of military uniforms in a short time led to great advances in clothes production, such as the creation of standard sizes.

Shortages in the South

The South had traditionally relied on mills in the North for manufactured cloth. When the war ended the trade, cloth prices rose in the Confederacy and there was a shortage of fabric. Cloth became unaffordable. In the fall of 1863, a dress that had cost $9 was $195 two years later.

Southern women learned to recycle fabric and to make their own dyes. In Margaret Mitchell's *Gone with the Wind*, Southern belle Scarlett O'Hara is so desperate that she uses living room drapes to make a dress. Women also used their tablecloths and

1861
July–September

CIVIL WAR

JULY 2, WISCONSIN Union forces push back Confederates near Hainesville in the Battle of Hoke's Run.

JULY 6, CUBA The Confederate raiding ship CSS *Sumter* captures seven Union vessels in Cuban waters.

JULY 21, VIRGINIA The first major battle of the war is fought at Manassas/First Bull Run. Confederates led by Pierre G.T. Beauregard defeat General Irvin McDowell's larger Union army.

OTHER EVENTS

JULY, UNITED STATES The Pony Express arrives in San Francisco, beginning a cross-country mail service.

JULY, UNITED STATES Congress approves the printing of the first dollar bills, known as "greenbacks."

July

bedlinen to make clothes, and they made their own dyes from trees and plants. Plantation women sometimes took back dresses they had given to their slaves. Many women resorted to spinning their own yarn to make "homespun." Before the war, this coarse fabric had been worn by slaves and poor whites. Now it became standard wear for Southern women.

As the war went on, Northern women also made economies, but they were not as severe as in the South. Wealthier Northern women continued to dress in the latest fashions. Southern women had once learned about the latest fashions from Europe: now they learned about them from the invading Union troops.

Shoe shortage

By the end of the war many Southerners could barely eat, let alone find new clothes. Women stitched shoes from cloth and paper, while children went barefoot. Some women could not leave the house because they had no shoes.

The Civil War drastically altered women's clothing in the South. As women of all classes used their initiative to clothe themselves and their families, clothing that had once been a highly visible indication of class became far more uniform.

Mary Todd Lincoln, the First Lady, wore this silk crinoline in 1861.

THE CRINOLINE

The crinoline skirt used a frame of hoops to create a shape that showed off a woman's small waist while also hiding the shape of her legs. It was originally popular with all social classes, but before the war the skirts had grown up to 5 feet (1.5 m) across. That required 20 yards (18 m) of fabric, meaning that only wealthy women could afford such a fashion. For working women, smaller hoops were more practical and cheaper. In the 1860s the skirt became narrower and flatter at the front, with the bulk at the back. It became more difficult to tell a woman's class by the style of her dress.

AUGUST 10, MISSOURI
The Battle of Wilson's Creek is the first major battle on the Mississippi River; it sees the first death of a Union general, Nathaniel Lyon.

SEPTEMBER 3, KENTUCKY
Confederate forces invade Kentucky, ending its neutrality.

SEPTEMBER 12–15, WEST VIRGINIA
General Robert E. Lee's Confederate forces are beaten at the Battle of Cheat Mountain Summit.

SEPTEMBER 19, KENTUCKY
The Battle of Barbourville sees Confederates raid an empty Union guerrilla training base.

AUGUST, UNITED STATES
The U.S. Government introduces the first income tax to raise funds for the war.

August   September

Country Life

The Civil War coincided with a revolution in rural life. Traditional farming was back-breaking work, but by the mid-19th century, new machines were increasingly freeing farmers from manual labor.

Cyrus McCormick (foreground) stands in front of his invention, the mechanical reaper.

In many ways the Civil War could be described as a farmers' war. The majority of soldiers were either farmers, or worked or lived on farms. Just before the war began, in 1860, more than half—58 percent—of the labor force worked on the country's two

1861
October–December

CIVIL WAR

OCTOBER 21, KENTUCKY 7,000 Union troops defeat Confederates at the Battle of Camp Wildcat on Wildcat Mountain.

OCTOBER 21, MISSOURI Union attempts to cross the Potomac River at Harrison's Island fail in the Battle of Ball's Bluff.

OCTOBER 21, MISSOURI The Union controls southeastern Missouri after the Battle of Fredericktown.

NOVEMBER 7, MISSOURI Ulysses S. Grant's Union forces defeat Confederates at the Battle of Belmont.

OTHER EVENTS

OCTOBER 22, UNITED STATES The first telegraph line is completed linking the east and west coasts.

NOVEMBER 1, CONFEDERACY Jefferson Davis is elected as president of the Confederacy.

October   November

million farms. Farmworkers included many women, who traditionally did jobs such as raising poultry and preserving food. When so many men left the farms to fight in the Civil War, their mothers, wives, and daughters often became responsible for all farm activities.

Life improves

In many ways, rural life was improving just before the war began. Many homes had better lighting, for example, thanks to the increased availability of kerosene lamps. The railroad network was expanding, which gave farmers the opportunity to sell to new markets.

With the start of the conflict, however, farmers in both the North and the South faced the challenge of increasing agricultural production to feed both soldiers and civilians. In the North, a combination of a shortage of workers and the chance to get high prices for their produce encouraged farmers to use mechanized equipment to reduce the amount of labor needed to produce crops and to increase production.

Slaves leave the fields to join the Union troops in the background. As slaves left their work, Southern farms struggled to keep up food production.

Technological breakthrough

The first breakthrough in increasing production had been invented by Cyrus McCormick in 1834. McCormick's mechanical reaper cut ripe wheat, a task that had previously been done by hand. By the time the war began, machines

NOVEMBER 8, CUBA The British steamer *Trent* is stopped by Union warship *San Jacinto* in an action that breaks international law, as Britain is not a combatant in the Civil War.

NOVEMBER 8, KENTUCKY The Battle of Ivy Mountain, also known as Ivy Creek, sees Union soldiers push Confederates back into Virginia.

DECEMBER 20, VIRGINIA Union troops defeat Confederate cavalry under J.E.B. "Jeb" Stuart in the Battle of Dranesville.

NOVEMBER 19, UNITED STATES Julia Howe writes the first verses of "The Battle Hymn of the Republic."

DECEMBER 14, GREAT BRITAIN Prince Albert, the husband of Queen Victoria, dies, plunging his wife into a long period of mourning.

LABOR SAVERS

The mechanized reaper encouraged the production of other machines that could increase production while at the same time making farmers' work easier. Such implements included grain drills that made holes for planting crops and horse-powered threshing machines, which separated the wheat grains from the rest of the stalk.

harvested about 70 percent of the wheat grown west of the Appalachians. Once war began, grain farmers without enough workers for the harvest were eager to buy new and improved reapers. In just one year, 1864, manufacturers produced 85,000 reapers: more than had been produced between the machine's invention in 1834 and 1861. When the war began, a reaper crew of 10 could harvest 10 to 12 acres (4 to 4.8 ha) per day; by the war's end, eight men could harvest 15 acres (6 ha) per day.

Thanks to such advances, Northern farmers not only fed the whole population but also exported food. In the 1850s, the United States had exported 8 million bushels of wheat a year; during the war, that figure rose to 27 million bushels a year.

Thanks to new technology, fruit and vegetables could be stored by being canned. Milk was also canned after it had been condensed, a method discovered by Gail Borden. Condensed milk gave dairy farmers a whole new market— and could be shipped over long distances to improve nutrition for Union soldiers.

The threshing machine made Northern farms far more productive.

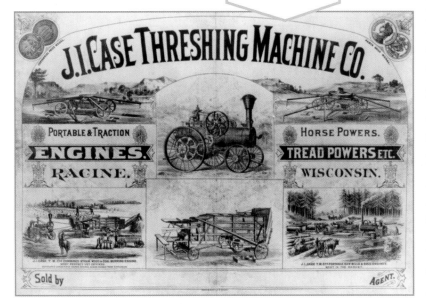

Life in the South

The technological advances in the North soon left farmers in the South behind. They had little access to new inventions. Fewer

1862
January–March

CIVIL WAR

JANUARY 18, ARIZONA
The Confederate Territory of Arizona is formed from part of what was the old Territory of New Mexico.

FEBRUARY 6, TENNESSEE
Union General Ulysses S. Grant takes the Confederate Fort Henry. The Tennessee River is now under Union control as far as Alabama.

FEBRUARY 16, TENNESSEE
Grant's troops take Fort Donelson; 15,000 Southerners surrender.

OTHER EVENTS

FEBRUARY, UNITED STATES "The Battle Hymn of the Republic" is published. It quickly becomes a popular marching song in the Union.

January   February

Slaves harvest wheat in the South. Many Southern farms still relied on hand labor rather than machines.

agricultural tools were made, because the government wanted factories to produce weapons instead. New tools became scarce. In addition, no machine had been invented that could harvest the main Southern crop, cotton. Some plantation owners resisted the introduction of new technology. They were worried that there would be less need for labor, which would reduce the value of their slaves.

Contrasting developments

Overall, farmers in the North used technology to produce more food for both domestic use and to sell. In the South, however, farmers struggled to replace cotton with food crops to feed their soldiers and civilians. When the war ended in 1865, Northern agriculture had undergone great change thanks to technology and the market economy. In the South, on the other hand, farmers and planters suffered from a lack of advances in technology and from the loss of slave labor.

COTTON IS KING

In 1860 Southern cotton made up half the value of all U.S. exports. The South produced 90 percent of the world's cotton. Once war began and the Northern blockade took effect, the cotton trade virtually stopped. It came to be seen as a patriotic duty to grow food instead of cotton to feed the new Confederacy. But politicians believed that cotton was a useful weapon. They even planned to withhold cotton so that America's trading partners would put pressure on the U.S. government to end the war and allow cotton exports to resume. But the plan did not work. There had been big cotton crops in 1859 and 1860. The world had enough cotton and did not have to depend on the South.

FEBRUARY 25, TENNESSEE With the loss of forts Henry and Donelson, Nashville is the first Confederate state capital to fall to Union forces.

MARCH 6–8, ARKANSAS The Confederates are defeated at the Battle of Pea Ridge, the largest battle on Arkansas soil.

MARCH 8–9, VIRGINIA The Battle of Hampton Roads sees Confederate and Union ironclads fight to a standstill.

MARCH 17, VIRGINIA The Union Army of the Potomac sails to Fort Monroe to begin the Peninsular Campaign.

MARCH, EAST AFRICA Zanzibar becomes an independent nation.

MARCH 10, UNITED STATES The first U.S. paper money goes into circulation.

Education and Literacy

In the years before the war, parts of the United States had some of the highest percentages in the world of people who could read. The picture varied dramatically across the country, however.

This school for black children was set up after the Union captured Charleston, South Carolina.

O ne basic difference was between North and South. Many Northern states had a system of public education that dated back to the 1830s. In parts of New England, for example, 75 percent of children went to school. (About 90 percent of

1862 April–June

CIVIL WAR

APRIL 6–7, TENNESSEE In the Battle of Shiloh Ulysses S. Grant narrowly defeats Confederate forces, with heavy losses on both sides.

APRIL 12, GEORGIA Union agent James Ambrose steals a Confederate train on the Western & Atlantic Railroad. He is captured and hanged.

APRIL 29, THE SOUTH The Confederacy passes a conscription act forcing men aged 18 to 50 to enlist in the army; many farms go into decline as farmers join up.

APRIL 29, LOUISIANA The Union occupation of New Orleans opens access to the rest of Louisiana and the Mississippi Valley.

OTHER EVENTS

APRIL 8 UNITED STATES Inventor John D. Lynde patents the first aerosol spray.

April

adults in the region could read and write.) There was a wide choice of schools, including fee-paying private schools and charity schools; there were also common schools, the forerunners of today's public schools. In some places, children who did not go to school during the week—perhaps because they had to work—could learn basic literacy at Sunday schools. In frontier areas without large villages or towns, children went to one-room schoolhouses or were educated by their parents.

In the South, education was less well established. Only one-third of white children there were enrolled in school. Their help was often needed on the farm or for other work, so on average they only attended school for three months a year. Only 80 percent of white adults were literate. Many people in the South mocked Northerners for the importance they placed on education. What use was teaching everyone, they asked, if most people would grow up to become subsistence farmers.

A Union soldier reads a newspaper. The Northern armies had a high level of literacy, and writing letters and reading were popular pastimes.

Educating African Americans

In the South, few black children were educated. Slave owners feared that educating slaves would encourage them to revolt. In the North, meanwhile, black children went to school, but separately from white children, apart from in Massachusetts. The school boards that handed out funds usually favored white schools, so black schools were often cold, poorly furnished, and short of books and other educational material. There were also some "Negro colleges" such as Avery College in Pittsburgh,

MAY 31, VIRGINIA
The Battle of Fair Oaks (Seven Pines) is drawn. Union losses are 5,050 and Confederate losses are 6,150.

JUNE 1, VIRGINIA
General Robert E. Lee takes command of the Army of Northern Virginia after General Joseph Johnston is wounded.

JUNE 12, VIRGINIA
J.E.B. Stuart and 1,200 cavalry raid the Union camp outside Richmond, taking 165 prisoners.

JUNE 25, VIRGINIA
The first battle of the Seven Days' Campaign— the Battle of Oak Grove—sees McClellan's Union forces halted near Richmond.

MAY 5, MEXICO
A Mexican army defeats an invading French force in the Battle of Puebla.

MAY 20, UNITED STATES
The Homestead Act makes millions of acres of Western land available to settlers.

May   June

which had been established in 1849 by the abolitionist Charles Avery.

During the war, attitudes toward the black population changed in many Northern states. After the war, funding improved for black education. In 1865, for example, Rhode Island desegregated its schools; it was followed in 1867 by Connecticut.

Mount St. Mary's College in Emmitsburg, Maryland, was a private Catholic university and school.

Progress was slow, however. Schools remained segregated in many Northern states until the end of the century.

In the South, slaves liberated by Union troops usually had some education provided by voluntary organizations. The Freedman's Aid organizations ran Negro schools on behalf of the government. During Reconstruction, Southern education remained strictly segregated. White schools received far more funding than schools for blacks.

Education and identity

In the years before and during the war, school classrooms played an important role in shaping the different identities of the Union and the Confederacy. In the North, for example, a deep sense of Protestant values underlay education, even outside of the Sunday School. Such values were summed up

A WOMAN'S WORLD

Before the Civil War, women were expected to stay at home. With so many men away fighting, women took their jobs, including as teachers. Most teachers during the Civil War were women. They usually taught several grades together, and were quick to beat children who were naughty.

1862 July–September

CIVIL WAR

JULY 1, WASHINGTON, D.C. The Union introduces an Internal Revenue Act, imposing a tax on income to raise money to pay for the war.

JULY 13, WASHINGTON, D.C. President Lincoln reads a draft of the Emancipation Proclamation to his cabinet.

JULY 17, THE NORTH The Confiscation Act and Militia Act come into force, opening the way for the creation of black regiments of freed slaves.

AUGUST 29, VIRGINIA The Second Battle of Bull Run (Manassas) begins.

OTHER EVENTS

JULY 4, GREAT BRITAIN Lewis Carroll makes up the story that will become *Alice in Wonderland* to amuse a young friend.

JULY 14, UNITED STATES Congress introduces the Medal of Honor for valor in the military services.

July   August

in books like *The New England Primer*, which children used in the classroom. They also had to memorize the federal catechism from *Webster's American Spelling Book*. This series of questions and answers stressed the importance of the U.S. Constitution. In the South, on the other hand, school textbooks promoted the virtues of the Confederacy and the importance of defending it against "Yankee" wrongs.

Education during wartime

When the war began, schools in the North largely carried on as normal, although some older students left to work in the fields or the factories. The shortage of male teachers also added to a trend that had already begun toward female domination of the teaching profession.

The impact of war was far greater on schools in the South. School enrollment fell as parents diverted school fees and older children replaced their fathers in the fields. Although teachers were not drafted, so many enlisted that schools had to close or to shorten their semesters.

In the North and the South, higher education institutions suffered from low numbers as their students enlisted. Casualty rates meant that many never returned to their studies.

A few children on both sides quit school to serve in the army, like this young Union soldier.

SLAVE EDUCATION

In the South, educating slaves had been generally discouraged. In a number of states it was illegal to teach slaves to read. Slaveholders believed that if slaves were literate, they would read abolitionist material that would encourage them to revolt. That did not prevent about 1 in 10 slaves learning some basic literacy skills, however. They were taught by free blacks, by other slaves, or by kindly whites. In particular, evangelical Christians often taught their slaves to read. In their faith it was vital for believers to have a personal connection with God—which could only be achieved by being able to read the Bible for themselves.

AUGUST 30, VIRGINIA
Confederate Robert E. Lee defeats the Union army at Bull Run. His casualties stand at 9,500, while Union losses are 14,500.

SEPTEMBER 17, MARYLAND
The Battle of Antietam ends in a draw after heavy losses on both sides: Lee's Army of Northern Virginia suffers 10,000 casualties; the Union Army of the Potomac loses 12,400 dead, wounded, or missing.

SEPTEMBER 22, WASHINGTON, D.C.
Lincoln issues a preliminary Emancipation Proclamation.

SEPTEMBER 24, TENNESSEE
Union General William Sherman orders the destruction of every house in Randolph in revenge for Confederate shelling of his steamboats.

AUGUST 18, UNITED STATES An uprising by young Sioux Indians in Minnesota leaves more than 800 white settlers dead.

Everyday Life

Lives in the United States in the 1860s varied hugely, depending on where people lived, whether they were male or female, and whether they were free or enslaved.

Factory chimneys smoke above a Pennsylvania town. The North was far more industrial and urban than the South.

The most important factor shaping daily life was where a person lived. The regions had their own different characters: the North was considered businesslike, the South gracious and elegant, and the West tough but honest.

1862 October–December

CIVIL WAR

OCTOBER 3, MISSISSIPPI
A Union army defeats the Confederates in the Battle of Corinth.

OCTOBER 11, VIRGINIA
The Confederate Congress passes an unpopular draft law that exempts anyone owning more than 20 slaves—the wealthiest part of society—from military service.

NOVEMBER 7, WASHINGTON, D.C.
Lincoln fires George B. McClellan as commander of the Army of the Potomac and appoints Ambrose E. Burnside in his place.

OTHER EVENTS

OCTOBER 8, PRUSSIA Otto von Bismarck becomes minister-president of Prussia; he uses his position to mastermind the unification of Germany.

NOVEMBER 4, UNITED STATES
Richard Gatling patents the machine gun that is named for him: the Gatling gun.

October   November

Northern life

In the North, most of the population of 22 million still lived in rural areas on farms and in small towns. Their lives were often very hard. Farmers and their families started work at dawn: they raised animals, sowed and harvested crops, did household chores, and preserved food for winter.

However, a growing number of Northerners were living in cities and towns of 20,000 inhabitants or more. In some ways their lives were easier, but cities were noisy, dirty, and smelly. They were also crowded. New immigrants from Europe often lived one family to a room as they began their lives in the "New World." Tenement blocks were packed with inhabitants. One outhouse in a central courtyard often served as a bathroom for an entire building. Most buildings were only four storys tall, although some taller buildings were being constructed.

HOME WASHING MACHINE & WRINGER.

New inventions such as this home washer helped make life in the North easier for many people.

Southern life

The most obvious difference between life in the North and the South was the existence of slavery in the South. In fact, only a minority of Southerners owned slaves, but slavery touched all

DECEMBER 7, TENNESSEE
Confederates defeat Union troops at the Battle of Hartsville, opening parts of western Tennessee and Kentucky.

DECEMBER 13–14, VIRGINIA
Burnside is beaten back in the Battle of Fredericksburg, with the loss of 6,500 Union troops.

DECEMBER 31, TENNESSEE
Union troops triumph in the Battle of Murfreesboro, taking Kentucky and increasing their hold on Tennessee.

DECEMBER 30, UNITED STATES
Lincoln reads his Emancipation Proclamation to his cabinet for comments.

DECEMBER 31, UNITED STATES
Lincoln signs an act admitting West Virginia to the Union.

LIFE IN FACTORIES

Many jobs in Northern cities were in factories and mills. Third and fourth generations of industrial workers made stovepipes, railroad engines, cloth, and thousands of other items. There were few unions or labor organizations to protect workers from unsafe conditions or to fight for better wages. Joining a union could be punished by being fired. The factory day began before dawn and ended 12 to 14 hours later, with half days on Saturday. Employers hired boys and girls to save on wages, so many urban children, often from immigrant families, never went to school.

parts of daily life. Slaveholders were the wealthiest people in the South, and they dominated local politics. Slavery also made it easy to see where someone fit in society. If you were black and lived in the South, you were probably a slave.

As in the North, Southern women were responsible for looking after the family. Educating children, looking after the home, preserving and cooking food, and medical care were all seen as women's duties. Black and white children played together until the ages of between four and seven, when black children were sent to work. Most black children worked in the fields with their parents. Some of them were taught a trade or craft and were put to work as an apprentice to a skilled worker. Others became house servants. Few were taught to read or write, because of fears that they might become politically active. As fears of slave uprisings increased throughout the first half of the century, slaves and free blacks were more and more restricted in their daily activities.

The basic furniture in this ship's cabin resembled that of homes throughout the United States.

Western life

In the West, an increasing number of settlers moved to regions west of the Mississippi River. Most of these settlers were farmers. They had been encouraged by the government to settle on land originally taken from Native Americans.

1863
January–March

CIVIL WAR

JANUARY 1, WASHINGTON, D.C.
The Emancipation Proclamation comes into effect, ruling that slaves in the South are free. The Civil War is now a war for the abolition of slavery, as well as a struggle to preserve the Union.

JANUARY 20–22, VIRGINIA
The Union Army of the Potomac tries to cross the Rappahannock River but turns back as rain turns the ground to mud.

OTHER EVENTS

JANUARY 1, UNITED STATES
The Homestead Act comes into law, encouraging western migration by granting land to farmers.

JANUARY 10, GREAT BRITAIN
The world's first underground railroad line opens in London.

FEBRUARY 3, UNITED STATES
Newspaper editor Samuel Clemens first uses the pen name by which he will become famous: Mark Twain.

January   **February**

Some settlers came under attack from native bands trying to claim back their territory. By the 1860s, however, attacks were less frequent, as native peoples had been pushed further west.

Life in the West was hard. The soil was poor for farming. Towns were small and far apart. Life could be very lonely, particularly for women used to being in close contact with their family. There were no modern conveniences to help with chores. In settled parts of the country, men and women had clearly divided tasks in the home. Such divisions were rare in the West: life was so hard that both men and women worked at whatever was necessary.

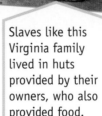

Slaves like this Virginia family lived in huts provided by their owners, who also provided food.

Limited roles

In the years before the Civil War, Americans' daily lives were defined by a range of limitations. One of the most important was race, which determined if they would be free or slave. Skin color also affected whether someone was educated or not, or poor or wealthy. Whether they were men or women shaped how involved in the larger world they became. The other major limitation was geographical: the way of life an American led depended on whether he or she lived in the North, South, or West of the nation.

A RIGID SOCIETY

In the South, black and white children were taught their place in society from an early age. Black children were taught to be careful how they talked to whites. They could be beaten or even arrested if they were seen as being rude or disrespectful. White children were taught that blacks were inferior. Slavery was good, because it "civilized" blacks and taught them Christianity. On both sides, teaching children such attitudes helped preserve the rigid social structure. Everyone had a defined place in society. That made it impossible for slaves—or even for poor whites—to escape from their allotted position as laborers for the upper classes.

MARCH 3, WASHINGTON, D.C.
The Union introduces the National Conscription Act, obliging men to join the army or pay $300 to hire a substitute.

MARCH 3, THE SOUTH
The Confederacy introduces an unpopular Impressment Act that allows army officers to take food from farmers at set rates.

FEBRUARY 24, UNITED STATES
Arizona is organized as a territory of the United States.

MARCH 3, UNITED STATES
The territory of Idaho is created.

Family Life

The American Civil War divided families, as relatives decided to support the Union or Confederate causes. The war is still often known as "the war between brothers."

A wedding is celebrated in a camp of the Army of the Potomac in 1863.

The Civil War had a lasting impact on all aspects of American life. It devastated families as fathers, brothers, and sons went off to fight—and often did not return. Other families found themselves caught up in the actual fighting, which raged across

1863
April–June

CIVIL WAR

APRIL 2, VIRGINIA
"Bread riots" break out in the Confederacy over the high price of food; the worst riots are in Richmond.

APRIL 17, MISSISSIPPI
Union cavalry raids Mississippi, tearing up railroad lines. Soldiers ride south to the Union city of Baton Rouge, Louisiana.

MAY 2–4, VIRGINIA The Confederate Army of Northern Virginia defeats the Union Army of the Potomac at the Battle of Chancellorsville; however, Confederate commander "Stonewall" Jackson is shot by one of his own men and dies.

MAY 14, MISSISSIPPI
Union troops capture Jackson, the fourth state capital to fall to Union troops.

OTHER EVENTS

MAY 22, UNITED STATES
The War Department establishes the Bureau of Colored Troops.

April   May

farms and towns. More lived close behind the front lines and found their homes pressed into service as supply bases or military headquarters. The churches and schools they atttended became makeshift military hospitals or morgues. But although many civilians were caught up in the war, family life—or a version of it—went on despite the carnage.

Role of women

In particular the war brought profound changes to the part women played in society, as a result of the great exodus of men to serve in the military. In the years before the war, life for the vast majority of American women was focused on the home and family. Before they were married, just 25 percent of white women worked outside the home; after marriage, that figure fell to only 5 percent.

Early in the conflict, women on both sides used traditional female skills to support the men; they sewed uniforms, cooked food, and tended minor injuries. As the war went on, however, they also took on more duties that had traditionally been carried out by men, such as chopping wood or fixing fences. Boys below the age of enlistment might share such tasks with their mothers or sisters. The shortage of available men meant that women were forced to take on responsibilities for which they had little or no practical experience. In addition to their work in the home, they took charge of their husbands' farms

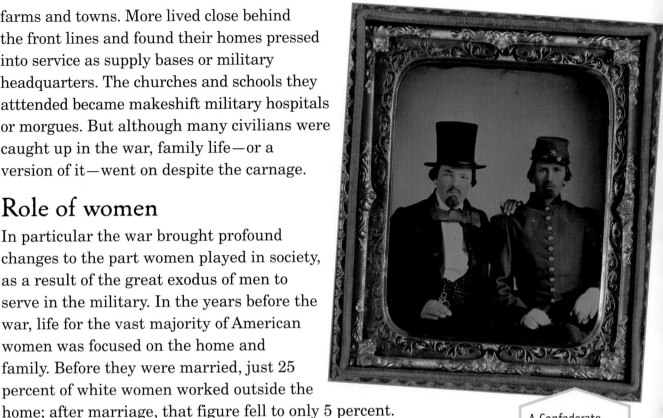

A Confederate soldier in uniform poses with his father. Many families were proud to send their sons to fight for the South.

MAY 18, MISSISSIPPI
Union armies begin the siege of Vicksburg.

JUNE 9, VIRGINIA
The Battle of Brandy Station ends in a Confederate victory.

JUNE 14, VIRGINIA
The Battle of Winchester is another Confederate victory.

JUNE 16, VIRGINIA
Lee orders the Army of Northern Virginia across the Potomac River to invade the North for a second time.

JUNE 28, WASHINGTON, D.C.
Lincoln replaces General Joseph Hooker as commander of the Army of the Potomac with General George Meade, whom he hopes will be more aggressive.

JUNE 7, MEXICO French troops capture Mexico City; the French want to begin a colony while Americans are distracted by the war.

JUNE 20, UNITED STATES
West Virginia is admitted to the Union following a presidential proclamation.

This popular print shows a Union soldier dreaming of being reunited with his family.

and businesses. They became laborers, plantation managers, and clerks. Many taught school. Before the war, only 7 percent of teachers in North Carolina were women; by its end, women made up over half of the state's teachers.

On the home front in the South, many towns came to be inhabited exclusively by white women, children, and slaves. As the war went on, many Southern women became responsible for managing the family's slaves.

LETTERS HOME

Many soldiers in the Civil War had never been away from home before. Keeping in contact with home was very important. Among Union troops, literacy was high; writing letters was one of the most popular uses of a soldier's free time. A friend could take dictation or read for those who were illiterate.

Death and divisions

The Civil War was the bloodiest conflict in U.S. history. More than 620,000 soldiers and an unknown number of civilians died. Such a large number of deaths touched almost every family in the country. Particularly in the South, there was scarcely a family that did not lose a son, brother, or father.

Families were not broken up only by death and grief. Many were divided by the principles that lay behind the conflict. Family members disagreed or fell out with one another; some ended up fighting one another. Even the president was affected. Abraham Lincoln's four brothers-in-law fought on the Confederate side. One of them was killed.

1863 July–September

CIVIL WAR

JULY 1–3, PENNSYLVANIA
The Battle of Gettysburg yields 20,000 casualties on each side in a decisive Union victory that marks a turning point in the war.

JULY 4, MISSISSIPPI
The fall of Vicksburg to the Union splits the Confederacy in two.

JULY 13, NEW YORK
Antidraft riots erupt across the North; in the worst, in New York City, African Americans are attacked and draft offices burned.

JULY 18, SOUTH CAROLINA
The 54th Massachusetts Volunteer Infantry, a black Union unit, fails in a courageous attack on Fort Wagner.

OTHER EVENTS

JULY 1, SOUTH AMERICA
The Dutch abolish slavery in their colony of Suriname.

JULY, CAMBODIA French writers reveal for the first time the existence of the remarkable ruined city of Angkor in the Cambodian jungle.

July

General Robert E. Lee had to make a difficult choice between his conscience and family ties. Lee had served in the U.S. Army for 30 years, following in the footsteps of his father, "Lighthorse" Harry Lee, a hero of the Revolutionary War. Yet at the start of the war, Lee turned down the offer of a command of the Union forces. He explained that, while he could not see what secession would achieve, he could not go against his native Virginia: "I could not raise my hand against my birthplace, my home, my children." He quit the U.S. Army and later became the most famous of all Confederate commanders.

Many other individuals faced the same predicament. Flora Cook, for example, was the daughter of a Union army general. But she was married to J.E.B. ("Jeb") Stuart, who gave up his commission in the U.S. army to join the Confederacy. Jeb asked Flora to move with their children to the Confederacy. To the horror of her strongly Unionist family, Flora agreed and moved to Saltville, Virginia.

Such individual moral dilemmas occurred again and again. The Civil War tore families apart not only through the deaths it caused. It also caused crises of conscience and principle, and family divisions that would not be reconciled for many years—if ever.

A slave is sold and separated from the rest of his family.

SLAVE FAMILIES

Although slave marriages were not recognized by law, many slaves married and raised families. Slave owners often encouraged slaves to have families. Since 1807, it had been forbidden to import slaves from Africa. Childbirth was therefore vital in order to add to slave numbers. Some slave owners allowed slave families to live together. Other owners tore families apart with little hesitation by selling or relocating one or more of their members. Campaigners against slavery highlighted the fact that as many as one in four slave families were broken up this way.

AUGUST 17, SOUTH CAROLINA Union forces begin a bombardment of Fort Sumter in Charleston Harbor, the place where the first shots of the war were fired.

AUGUST 20, KANSAS William Quantrill's Confederate guerrillas attack Lawrence, killing more than 150 civilians and destroying 200 buildings.

SEPTEMBER 19–20, TENNESSEE Confederates win a hollow victory at the two-day Battle of Chickamauga, losing 18,000 to the Union's 16,000, and forcing only a partial Union withdrawal to Chattanooga.

SEPTEMBER 29, ITALY Troops led by the nationalist Giuseppe Garibaldi defeat a papal army, a major obstruction to Italian unification.

Food and Drink

The farms of the United States had always been able to feed the country's population. After war began, however, the situation soon changed. The South suffered from shortages and high prices.

Union troops gather at a cookhouse. There were no army cooks: small groups of men cooked for each other.

The situation varied dramatically between the North and the South. In the North, for example, Union troops enjoyed a Thanksgiving feast in November 1864. The public sent the soldiers turkeys, ham, beef, or oysters.

1863
October–December

CIVIL WAR

OCTOBER 15, SOUTH CAROLINA
Confederate submarine *H.L. Hunley* sinks on its second test voyage, drowning all its crew.

NOVEMBER 19, PENNSYLVANIA
Lincoln makes his famous "Gettysburg Address" during the dedication of the cemetery on the battlefield.

OTHER EVENTS

OCTOBER 3, UNITED STATES
President Abraham Lincoln proclaims the last Thursday in November as Thanksgiving Day.

OCTOBER 23, SWITZERLAND
The first conference of the International Committee of the Red Cross is held.

NOVEMBER 23, UNITED STATES
A patent is granted to the first process for color photography.

October   November

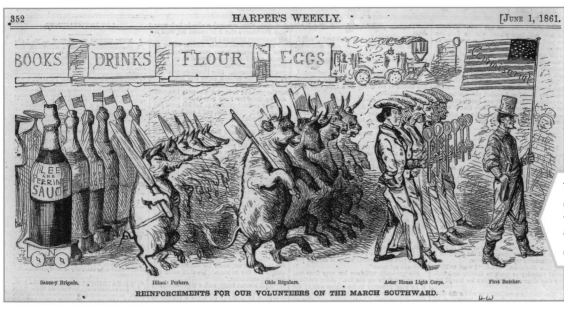

852   HARPER'S WEEKLY.   [JUNE 1, 1861.

BOOKS   DRINKS   FLOUR   EGGS

Sauce-y Brigade.   Illinois Porkers.   Ohio Regulars.   Astor House Light Corps.   First Butcher.

REINFORCEMENTS FOR OUR VOLUNTEERS ON THE MARCH SOUTHWARD.

This 1861 Union cartoon shows "reinforcements" in the shape of cattle and hogs.

Southern home front

In the South, things were very different. Civilians could barely feed themselves, let alone donate food for a feast. By the summer of 1861, only months after the start of the war, the Union blockade of Southern ports began to take effect. Farmers began to hoard their crops, both to feed their own families and in order to sell later for higher profits. From 1862 food shortages and so-called "bread riots" became common across the Confederacy.

By 1863 people had become used to going hungry. Even basic foodstuffs were in short supply. Meat had almost disappeared from the daily diet throughout the South, together with butter and milk. Even the rich were living on cornbread—although corn was growing expensive—sugar, and flour.

NOVEMBER 23, TENNESSEE
The Battle of Chattanooga sees Union troops push back the Confederates.

NOVEMBER 24–25, TENNESSEE The Union capture of Chattanooga opens the "Gateway to the South."

DECEMBER 1, WASHINGTON, D.C.
Confederate spy Belle Boyd is freed from prison by Union authorities.

DECEMBER 9, TENNESSEE
After a 16-day siege, Confederate defenders withdraw from the town of Knoxville.

DECEMBER 16, TENNESSEE General Joseph Johnston takes command of the Confederate Army of Tennessee, replacing General William Hardee.

NOVEMBER 26, UNITED STATES
The first modern Thanksgiving Day is celebrated in the North.

DECEMBER 1, CHILE
A fire in a church causes panic in which 1,500 worshipers die.

This drawing shows a female sutler selling provisions from a covered wagon.

A MOVEABLE FEAST

Soldiers could buy food from sutlers. These licensed traders followed the armies in wagons to sell provisions to the men. They also sold beer and whiskey, even though troops were forbidden to drink alcohol. The food was often prepared in unhygienic conditions and made soldiers sick.

Coffee, the standard drink, soon ran out. People tried various substitutes, such as corn and even cotton. They discovered that none of them tasted much like coffee.

Families who lived in the country were somewhat better off than those in towns, because they could grow and eat their own food. However, it became harder to find enough laborers to plant and harvest the crops. Toward the end of the war many Southerners were hungry, and women and children were often malnourished and underweight.

Soldiers' food

The restrictions in diet eventually had an impact on Southern troops as well as on civilians. In the North, meanwhile, crops were harvested and distributed as usual. Food was preserved in the recently invented tin can, made in thousands by Northern factories. Union troops were issued with new products such as condensed milk. Some men in the Union army had never eaten so well.

In both the armies the basic food rations included hardtack, beef, beans, and coffee, but Union ration supplies remained pretty constant throughout the war. Those in the South gradually dwindled as the war went on.

The staple food for all the troops was hardtack. It was a dry biscuit like a cracker, usually made from flour, salt, and water.

1864 January–March

CIVIL WAR

JANUARY 14, GEORGIA Union General William T. Sherman begins his infamous March through the South.

JANUARY 17, TENNESSEE At the Battle of Dandridge, Confederate forces repel Union troops from the Dandridge area.

FEBRUARY 9, VIRGINIA A total of 109 Union prisoners escape through a tunnel at Libby Prison in Richmond.

FEBRUARY 14–20, MISSISSIPPI In the Battle of Meridian, William T. Sherman leads a successful Union raid to destroy an important railroad junction.

OTHER EVENTS

FEBRUARY 1, DENMARK Prussian forces invade the Danish province of Schleswig, beginning the Second Schleswig War.

January

February

In the South it was frequently made from cornmeal. The bread was difficult to digest, so soldiers soaked it in coffee or soup or fried it in bacon grease. It was so common for the bread to be full of weevils that soldiers often joked that weevils were their main source of meat. Fresh meat was often in short supply, although armies sometimes had herds of cattle that they slaughtered for food. Otherwise, troops were supplied with salted beef or pork. The meat was often rotten, and it made soldiers sick or sometimes even killed them.

Substitute foods

Coffee had become popular shortly before the war. For soldiers, as for civilians, it was the most important drink. The North made sure to buy the best possible coffee for its troops. In the South, however, the Union blockade meant coffee was rare. Southerners had to pay high prices or make do with one of the poor coffee substitutes.

There were various ways for troops to supplement their rations. One of the most popular was foraging, or gathering produce from the countryside. Commanders on both sides led expeditions to find supplementary provisions. Such foraging often left civilians with reduced supplies of food, however.

This 1862 drawing shows a Union foraging party returning to camp with its supplies.

STARVING TROOPS

An officer in the Confederate Army of Northern Virginia described the soldiers' food situation in spring 1865: "There was an appalling and well-founded fear of starvation.... From the beginning ... our food supply had been barely sufficient to sustain life, and on the march from Spotsylvania to Cold Harbor ... three hard biscuits and one very meager slice of fat pork were issued to each man on our arrival, and that was the first food any of us had seen since our halt two days before. The next supply did not come until two days later, and it consisted of a single cracker per man, with no meat at all."

FEBRUARY 20, FLORIDA Many men of the 8th Regiment of United States Colored Troops are killed or injured in the Battle of Olustee near Jacksonville; Union forces retreat to the coast.

MARCH 2, THE NORTH Lieutenant General Ulysees S. Grant is made commander of all the armies of the United States.

MARCH 25, KENTUCKY Confederate cavalry attack the city of Paducah on the Ohio River; they retreat the next day, having suffered many casualties.

MARCH 14, AFRICA British explorers Samuel and Florence Baker discover Lake Albert at the headwaters of the Nile River.

Home Front in the South

The war transformed life in the South forever. It did not just bring an end to slavery: It was also a far more disruptive experience for many Southerners than for their Northern counterparts.

Women sew clothes for Confederate soldiers in 1864. By that time, many soldiers' uniforms were in tatters.

When the war began in 1861, most Southerners believed that the conflict would be short and that a Southern victory would be quickly achieved. They welcomed the war enthusiastically. They believed in the justice of their cause.

1864 April–June

CIVIL WAR

APRIL 12, TENNESSEE Confederate troops massacre the Union garrison at Fort Pillow, killing 202 African Americans.

APRIL 17, GEORGIA Hungry citizens of Savannah stage bread riots over the lack of food.

MAY 3, VIRGINIA The Union Army of the Potomac starts to move south, crossing the difficult terrain of the Wilderness region.

OTHER EVENTS

APRIL 10, MEXICO The French proclaim Archduke Maximilian of Austria to be emperor of Mexico.

APRIL 22, UNITED STATES Congress decides to print the phrase "In God We Trust" on U.S. coins.

MAY 9, NORTH SEA Austria and Denmark fight a naval battle at Heligoland during the Second Schleswig War.

April   May

Few people anticipated the wartime scarcities and hardships they would later have to endure. Women were willing to make sacrifices for the Confederate cause. They often encouraged men to do the same by enlisting immediately to fight for Southern independence.

Three out of every four eligible men left the South to serve in the Confederate army. That left the home front as a world dominated by women, children, and slaves. Women threw themselves into supporting the fighting men. They sewed flags and clothes, raised money, and set up hospitals and relief associations to help wounded soldiers.

In some parts of Southern society support for the war was not so enthusiastic. Some poorer white men were reluctant to join the army. The white planter elite dismissed such hesitation as cowardice, refusing to accept that it might reflect political beliefs. For their part, the planters kept faith in the Confederate cause until the end of the war.

Starving citizens of New Orleans rush for bread from Union authorities after the fall of the city.

Changing women's roles

When their husbands and sons went away to fight, women often had to take charge of family farms, and plantation owners' wives had to run the plantations. It was usually slave management that caused most problems for these planter-class women. Mistresses did not command the same authority as

MAY 5–6, VIRGINIA
Grant and Lee fight the inconclusive Battle of the Wilderness.

MAY 12, VIRGINIA
Grant and Lee fight again at the Battle of Spotsylvania. The battle is drawn.

JUNE 3, VIRGINIA
The Battle of Cold Harbor is a disaster for the Union army. They lose 7,000 men for no gain against Confederate losses of 1,500.

JUNE 27, GEORGIA
The Battle of Kennesaw Mountain sees Sherman's Union troops suffer heavy losses of 3,000 against Johnston's Confederate losses of 552.

MAY, GREAT BRITAIN
Charles Dickens publishes the first part of *Our Mutual Friend.*

MAY 26, UNITED STATES
Congress creates the territory of Montana, with its original capital at Virginia City.

JUNE 15, UNITED STATES Secretary of War Edwin M. Stanton creates Arlington National Cemetery, Virginia, on land previously owned by Confederate General Robert E. Lee.

June

SIEGE OF VICKSBURG

The diary of an anonymous lady described conditions faced by citizens during the siege of Vicksburg: "March 20th. The slow shelling ... goes on all the time, and we have grown indifferent. Noncombatants have been ordered to leave [the city] or prepare accordingly. Those who are to stay are having caves built.... Two diggers worked at ours a week and charged $30. It is well made in the hill that slopes just in the rear of the house.... When we went in this evening and sat down, the earthy, suffocating feeling, as of a living tomb, was dreadful to me."

masters. Slaves began to ignore their orders, or to run away to the Union lines. Some whites found it difficult to understand such changes in their slaves: it did not occur to them that their slaves might want a different outcome in the war.

Early in the war the Confederate government passed a law that excused a white man—a master or an overseer—from military service on any plantation that had more than 20 slaves. Those poorer families who did not have slaves, and whose women were left to work in the fields, resented what they saw as a law that favored the wealthy.

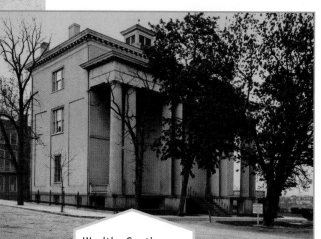

Wealthy Southerners had comfortable homes like this mansion belonging to President Jefferson Davis.

Hardship

Once the Union blockade began to take effect in 1862, some farm produce was in very short supply. Soon, thousands of acres of cotton fields were converted to grow staple crops. But growing food was often not the only problem. Just as important was the lack of a system to distribute food where it was needed. Iron, for example, was imported, so the South could not replace destroyed railroads.

Meanwhile, the Confederate currency became worth less and less. Prices rose more than sevenfold. This kind of inflation meant that people could not afford even basic foods.

1864
July–September

CIVIL WAR

JULY 9, MARYLAND Confederates defeat Union troops at the Battle of Monocacy.

JULY 11, WASHINGTON, D.C. Facing strong Union defenses, Confederates withdraw from their attack on the Union capital.

JULY 22, GEORGIA Confederate General Hood's troops fail to defeat General Sherman's men at the Battle of Atlanta. Confederate losses are 8,000; Union losses are 3,600.

AUGUST 5, ALABAMA Union warships defeat Confederate vessels at the Battle of Mobile Bay. Union admiral David G. Farragut is said to have ordered, "Damn the torpedoes; full speed ahead!"

OTHER EVENTS

JULY 5, UNITED STATES The Bank of California is founded with holdings of $2 million.

JULY 14, UNITED STATES Gold is discovered in Montana at Helena, which will later become the state capital.

AUGUST 8, SWITZERLAND The first Geneva Convention is held to discuss the treatment of wounded soldiers in war.

July   August

Fleeing from home

Much of the fighting took place on Southern territory. Families fled homes and farms that lay in the path of invading troops or of destructive campaigns. At least 250,000 Southerners were displaced from their homes. Many of these refugees headed for cities such as Richmond, Columbia, and Atlanta. When they got there, however, they often found housing and food were already in short supply.

Despair and defeat

As Union forces moved deeper into Southern territory, poorer Southerners were driven to despair. Thousands of soldiers deserted; they went home to try to help their families. Few records survive of how the poor reacted to the end of the war. The elite, on the other hand, were quick to express their grief and bitterness at the South's defeat. The legend developed of a Lost Cause: an idyllic way of life that had been destroyed by the war because the North did not understand Southern values. The South had never been defeated in a fair fight on the battlefield, this view argued. It had been ground down by the industry and finance of the merciless North.

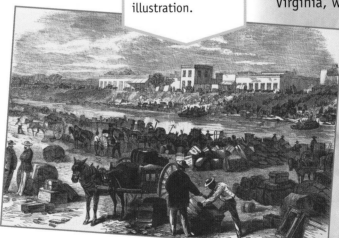

Confederates evacuate the port of Brownsville, Texas, in this 1864 illustration.

RIOTING FOR BREAD

As shortages became more common, protests spread across the South. By spring 1863 crops from the previous year's harvest were running out. Prices had risen out of control. People thought that storekeepers and the government were hoarding supplies. In more than a dozen places, starving women staged what were known as bread riots. The worst was in Richmond, Virginia, where rioters smashed store windows and seized goods. President Jefferson Davis tried to calm the situation, but the women only left after he threatened them with violence.

AUGUST 31, ILLINOIS The Democratic National Convention in Chicago nominates General George B. McClellan as its presidential candidate on an antiwar ticket.

SEPTEMBER 1, GEORGIA General Sherman cuts the last supply line to Atlanta, the railroad, forcing the Confederates to leave the city.

SEPTEMBER 16, VIRGINIA Confederate cavalrymen raid Union beef supplies on the James River to feed hungry Southerners.

SEPTEMBER 22, VIRGINIA Union forces defeat Confederates at the Battle of Fisher's Hill and start to destroy crops in the Shenandoah Valley.

SEPTEMBER 5, JAPAN British, Dutch, and French fleets attack Japan to open the Shimonoseki Straits to navigation.

SEPTEMBER 15, ITALY The new country gives up its claims to Rome; the Italians agree to make Florence their capital.

Home Front in the North

Compared to things in the South, life in the North continued much
as normal. There was little fighting there, a smaller proportion of
men were away at the war, and few people went hungry.

This illustration
shows the facilities
provided for Union
troops by volunteers
in Philadelphia.

The way the Union home front coped with the war was to
some extent inevitable. The North had far more resources
than the South in terms of both its population and its economy.
But the war effort also had to be managed well in terms of

1864
October–November

CIVIL WAR

OCTOBER 19, VIRGINIA
Union forces, under
General Sheridan, defeat
General Early's Confederate
Army of the Valley at the
Battle of Cedar Creek.

OCTOBER 26, ALABAMA
Union forces at Decatur prevent
Confederates led by John Bell
Hood from crossing the
Tennessee River in an attempt
to cut William T. Sherman's
lines of communication.

OCTOBER 27, VIRGINIA
Union forces assaulting
the Confederate capital
at Richmond are defeated
in the Second Battle of
Fair Oaks.

OTHER EVENTS

OCTOBER 11, UNITED STATES
Slavery is abolished
in Maryland.

OCTOBER 30, AUSTRIA The
Peace of Vienna ends the
Second Schleswig War between
Germany and Denmark.

OCTOBER 31, UNITED STATES
Nevada is admitted to the
Union as the 36th state.

October

public opinion to make sure that morale remained high and that people supported the Union cause. The North's advantage over the South began with its population.

The South had a total of only about 9 million citizens; the North's population was over 22 million. Only 5.4 million Southerners were white; the others were 3.5 million black slaves and 133,000 free blacks, neither of which could take part in the war. The North had 430,000 black slaves living in the states along the border with the South, plus 248,000 free blacks. The remaining 21.6 million citizens were white. In the South, most people worked at farming and other agricultural jobs. The North had far more industry and manufacturing, so its population had a much wider range of occupations.

Morale and the war effort

Responsibility for morale lay with individual states and local communities. Recruitment was carried out on a local level. At the start of the war, so many Northerners rushed to enlist that state governors asked the federal government to enlarge their quotas. During the war the Union raised some two million men, including more than 180,000 African Americans.

The men and women on the home front supported the war effort

This picture shows Wall Street, New York, in 1847. The city was already the nation's financial capital.

BURNING A NEW YORK ORPHANAGE

The riot that broke out in New York in July 1863 began as a protest against the draft. Soon, however, rioters' targets spread to include African Americans, who the rioters somehow blamed for causing the war. Many blacks were killed. Here, an eyewitness relates how rioters burned down an orphanage for African American children:
"The few [police] officers who stood guard over the doors ... were beaten down while the vast crowd rushed in.... The little ones, many of them beaten— all, orphans and caretakers, exposed to every indignity and every danger [were] driven on to the street, [and] the building was fired."

NOVEMBER 4, TENNESSEE
Confederate cavalry commander Nathan B. Forrest completes a 23-day raid in Georgia and Tennessee by destroying a Union supply base at Johsonville.

NOVEMBER 15, GEORGIA
Union general William T. Sherman burns much of Atlanta before setting out on his notorious "March to the Sea."

NOVEMBER 25, NEW YORK
Confederate spies fail in a plot to burn down New York City.

NOVEMBER 8, UNITED STATES
Abraham Lincoln is reelected for a second term as president of the United States.

NOVEMBER 29, UNITED STATES
Militia in Colorado massacre some 200 Cheyenne and Arapaho at Sand Creek in retaliation for an attack on settlers.

FUNDS FOR THE SOLDIERS

In many Northern cities, supporters raised money to help buy medicines and promote hygienic conditions for the troops. One of the most popular ways to raise funds was the "sanitary fair." The first was held in Chicago for two weeks in the fall of 1863. Some 5,000 visitors a day paid the 75-cent fee to attend. The fair's main attraction was the original draft of the Emancipation Proclamation. The draft was donated by President Lincoln and sold at auction for $3,000. In all, the fair raised $100,000. Other major cities held sanitary fairs of their own. The largest took place in New York in April 1864.

by making sure that the economy was healthy. The men who stayed home home to manage farms or work in factories were joined by a growing number of women. Most women worked as unskilled laborers, but the war gave them a chance to do jobs from which they had previously been barred.

A mob lynches an African American in the New York draft riot in July 1863.

Strikes and riots

The Union home front was not completely calm, however. During the war, prices rose quicker than wages. Workers found themselves unable to buy as much for their money. Some went on strike, but the strikes rarely won higher wages.

In March 1863, a draft was introduced in the Union, so that men could now be forced to join the army. It was possible to buy one's way out of the draft by paying a fee of $300—and many wealthier men did just that. That became a source of discontent for draftees who could not afford the money. In several places this discontent turned to violence. Some officials who tried to enforce the draft were murdered. At least 105 people were killed in a riot that broke out in New York City in July 1863. Angry mobs smashed up draft offices. They also murdered dozens of free blacks: they blamed black slaves for starting the war they were being forced to fight in.

1864–1865
December–January

CIVIL WAR

DECEMBER 13, GEORGIA
Union troops capture Fort McAllister near Savannah.

DECEMBER 15, TENNESSEE
At the Battle of Nashville, the Confederate Army of Tennessee is defeated by the Union Army of the Cumberland.

DECEMBER 20, GEORGIA
The Confederate garrison escapes from Savannah.

DECEMBER 21, GEORGIA
Sherman and his men enter Savannah unopposed at the conclusion of the March to the Sea.

OTHER EVENTS

DECEMBER 8, VATICAN Pope Pius IX publishes the Syllabus of Errors, which condemns liberalism and reformism.

December

Politics and patriotism

Politics continued during wartime, with the Democratic Party challenging the governing Republicans. The Democrats were divided, however. Most Democrats supported a war to preserve the Union, although many wanted to negotiate peace. But virtually all opposed measures they thought violated the U.S. Constitution, including emancipation and conscription. Both parties set up organizations to publish propaganda to make their views more widely known.

Life in the border states

The part of the Union where the war had most impact was in the border states. Families here were often split by their loyalties. Although Kentucky tried to remain neutral, once the fighting began, it was invaded by both Confederate and Union troops. In Maryland, parts of the state were under Union occupation, state elections were fixed against candidates who supported secession, and civilians were imprisoned without trial. Missouri suffered 1,162 battles and skirmishes (only Virginia and Tennessee saw more). Missourians were also terrorized by the violent activities of bands of both pro-Union and pro-Confederate guerrillas.

African Americans build defenses to protect a railroad in Virginia in 1861.

BENEVOLENT SOCITIES

Throughout the North, volunteer organizations were formed to support the war effort. They were supported by huge numbers of Union citizens. The bodies included Soldiers' Aid Associations, which raised funds to help troop welfare, collected supplies, and donated facilities. Another key body was the U.S. Sanitary Commission, which promoted hygiene and medical care in the field. The commission paid agents to inspect military camps and also sent doctors and ambulances on campaign with the armies.

JANUARY 15, NORTH CAROLINA
Wilmington, the last port in Confederate hands, is closed.

JANUARY 19, SOUTH CAROLINA
General Sherman vows to march through the Carolinas.

JANUARY 31, VIRGINIA
Robert E. Lee is named general-in-chief of all the Confederate armies.

JANUARY 4, UNITED STATES
The New York Stock Exchange opens its first permanent headquarters.

JANUARY 27, PERU
Peru's independence is established in a treaty with Spain.

JANUARY 31, UNITED STATES The House of Representatives approves an amendment to the Constitution abolishing slavery; it will become the Thirteenth Amendment.

Town and City Life

More people in the North lived in cities than in the South. While some Northern cities boomed during the war, Southern cities suffered shortages, or were occupied or put under siege.

A crowd of people in New York City eagerly read the latest headlines about the war.

I n 1860 only one tenth of Southerners lived in towns and cities. In the Union, urban dwellers made up one quarter of the population. For those Northerners, the war often seemed quite distant. The only cities that were ever under immediate

1865
February–March

CIVIL WAR

FEBRUARY 3, VIRGINIA
President Lincoln and Confederate representatives fail to agree a diplomatic ending to the war.

FEBRUARY 16, SOUTH CAROLINA
Columbia surrenders to General Sherman's Union troops.

FEBRUARY 17, SOUTH CAROLINA
As Union troops enter Columbia, someone sets fire to cotton bales. Over half of the city is destroyed in a huge blaze.

FEBRUARY 27, KENTUCKY
Confederate guerrilla leader William C. Quantrill and his band attack civilians in Hickman.

OTHER EVENTS

FEBRUARY 12, UNITED STATES
Henry Highland Garnet becomes the first African American to speak in the House of Representatives.

FEBRUARY 22, UNITED STATES
Tennessee adopts a new state constitution that outlaws slavery.

February

threat of attack were Washington, D.C., and Philadelphia at the time of the Battle of Gettysburg in July 1863. Many citizens of New York, Boston, and Chicago prospered from an unprecedented economic boom. In Southern cities, things were very different. War was never far from the Confederate capital, Richmond. Along the Mississippi River, cities such as Nashville, Vicksburg, and New Orleans were under Union occupation by 1863.

Riots in the North

But even in Northern cities, life was not entirely normal. Many men were away fighting. There were also shortages. Above all, there was a deep tension about the relations between different parts of society. Throughout the war, tensions in New York City spilled over into violence. In July 1863 police lost control of a riot against the draft law, and rioters killed more than a hundred people, mainly black Americans.

The cause of the violence lay in old tensions and hatreds that had been inflamed by the war. At the time, New York had 800,000 inhabitants. About one-quarter of New Yorkers were uneducated and unskilled Irish immigrants. They lived in overcrowded and insanitary slums in lower Manhattan and did menial jobs, such as road building or dockside labor. That brought them into competition for work with the city's

The Brooklyn Sanitary Fair was held in 1864 in a theater. The event raised money to support Union troops.

MARCH 2, VIRGINIA
The Shenandoah Valley is in Union control after the Confederates lose the Battle of Waynesboro.

MARCH 3, WASHINGTON, D.C. The U.S. Congress sets up the Freedmen's Bureau to help deal with the problems resulting from the sudden freeing of tens of thousands of slaves.

MARCH 13, VIRGINIA
The Confederate Congress passes a law authorizing the use of black troops.

MARCH 19, NORTH CAROLINA
Joseph E. Johnston attempts to stop the march of Union general William T. Sherman through the Carolinas in the Battle of Bentonville; he is defeated late the following day.

MARCH 4, UNITED STATES
Abraham Lincoln is inaugurated for his second term as president.

MARCH 18, SOUTH AMERICA
Paraguay goes to war with the Triple Alliance of Brazil, Argentina, and Uruguay.

New Yorkers ice skate in Brooklyn in 1862. In much of the North, life went on as usual.

HARD TIMES

Life in the South was much harder than in the North. In Richmond, Virginia, women who had lived in luxury before the war found themselves reduced to cutting up their fine gowns from Paris and selling them in small pieces to be made into bonnets in order to put basic food on the table.

population of poor blacks. The Irish took their frustrations out on these blacks. The New York riot was not so much about the draft itself as it was about Irish anger and resentment.

There was no doubt, however, that many poor Northerners did object to the draft law. They believed the draft was unfair because it made it possible for a man to buy his way out of the army—but only if he were wealthy. Those city-dwellers who could afford it saw nothing wrong in paying the exemption fee or hiring a substitute to fight in their place. They carried on as though there was no war.

The gap between rich and poor steadily grew. For most people, price rises left them a little poorer than before. Those who traded in arms and war supplies, meanwhile, made huge profits. For all these reasons the mood of many people on the streets of New York, and in some other cities of the Union, was surly and defensive.

Life in the capital

Unlike New Yorkers, citizens of Washington, D.C., became used to living with the threat of war. The city was prepared for invasion or siege from the First Battle of Bull Run in July 1861

1865
April–May

CIVIL WAR

APRIL 1, VIRGINIA
The Battle of Five Forks ends in defeat for the Confederate Army of Northern Virginia.

APRIL 2, VIRGINIA
Grant attacks Petersburg and the Confederates start a retreat from Petersburg and Richmond.

APRIL 6, VIRGINIA
Lee loses 8,000 men to Union attacks at the Battle of Sayler's Creek.

APRIL 7, VIRGINIA
Grant asks Lee for his army's surrender; Lee asks for terms.

APRIL 9, VIRGINIA
Lee surrenders to Ulysses S. Grant at Appomattox Courthouse.

OTHER EVENTS

April

until July 1864, when a corps of the Army of Northern Virginia had the capital in its sights. The city effectively became a huge military base. Everything was secondary to military needs. The Mall was full of makeshift field hospitals, where many of the city's women helped look after wounded soldiers. There were frequent outbreaks of disease, thanks to the presence of so many sick and wounded men. Under such circumstances, it was impossible to maintain even basic standards of hygiene.

Southern cities

In the South, city life was very difficult. The Union blockade had halted all imports, which created shortages and huge price rises. As a result, living standards plunged for everybody. With nearly every able-bodied white man in the army, women took on the responsibility of providing for themselves and their families.

Many people in Confederate cities accepted that it was necessary to make sacrifices for the war effort. There was discontent, however. The most serious outbreak occurred in April 1863, when a hungry mob went on a rampage in Richmond demanding bread. They looted clothing and jewelry stores, as well as bakeries and food stores.

Starving people in New Orleans rush to be fed by handouts from the U.S. authorities.

NEW ORLEANS

New Orleans spent most of the war under Union occupation. To begin with, the city was run by Union General Benjamin F. Butler. The citizens soon came to refer to him as "Beast" Butler. He provoked fury with his "Women's Order." Some women in the city showed open contempt for Union soldiers by spitting at them—or even by emptying chamber pots over them. Butler stated that women who were rude to the Union soldiers would be dealt with as if they were prostitutes. In late 1862, he was replaced by the less controversial General Nathaniel P. Banks.

APRIL 14, WASHINGTON, D.C.
President Lincoln is shot while watching a play at the theater.

APRIL 15, WASHINGTON, D.C.
Lincoln dies from his injuries; Vice-President Andrew Johnson becomes president.

APRIL 26, NORTH CAROLINA
Confederate General Joseph E. Johnston surrenders to General William T. Sherman.

MAY 10, GEORGIA
Confederate President Jefferson Davis is captured and taken into custody.

MAY 29, WASHINGTON, D.C.
President Andrew Johnson grants an amnesty and pardon to Confederate soldiers who will take an oath of allegiance to the Constitution.

APRIL 21, UNITED STATES
Lincoln's funeral train leaves Washington, D.C.; Lincoln's body is carried in a Pullman sleeping car.

APRIL 27, UNITED STATES 2,000 Union soldiers aboard the riverboat Sultana die when it catches fire and sinks on the Mississippi River in Tennessee.

MAY 1, UNITED STATES
Walt Whitman publishes "Drum Taps," his long poem about the Civil War.

NEED TO KNOW

Some of the subjects covered in this book feature in many state curricula. These are topics you should understand.

Resources:
Sources of labor
Food supplies
Weapons and ammunition
Southern cotton

Confederacy:
Bread riots
Women's roles
Shortages and inflation
Slavery

Union:
Draft riots
Economic reforms
Public opinion
Daily life

KNOW THIS

This section summarizes two major themes of this book: the Confederacy's struggle for resources, and daily life in both the North and the South.

RESOURCES

FOOD
By the middle of 1862 the Union blockade was severely restricting the imports of food on which the South relied. Southern farming was too heavily based on cotton to switch easily to producing food.

AGRICULTURE
During the war, the absence of male farmers, the destruction of fields by Union soldiers, and the decision of many slaves to stop working made it difficult for the South to feed all of its people; in the North, machines helped farms grow more productive.

PRICES
The Union and the Confederacy both printed money to pay for the war, which also made prices rise. In the North, inflation was 80 percent by the end of the war; in the South, rising prices combined with shortages to produce an inflation rate of 9,000 percent.

LABOR
In the South so many men joined the army that women had to do many jobs from which they had traditionally been excluded; the same thing happened in the North but to a far smaller extent, because the North's greater population meant that a smaller proportion of male workers went to fight.

DAILY LIFE

- How an American lived during the Civil War depended largely on where he or she lived.
- For many people in the North, life went on in many ways as normal; in the South, on the other hand, the war had a far more immediate impact on a greater share of the population.
- In the North, riots over the military draft were really an expression of tension between different ethnic groups.
- Civilians in the South suffered three main kinds of shortages: food to eat, goods such as clothing, and labor to work in the fields or in the few Southern manufacturing businesses.
- The North had far more factories and far more productive farms than the South.
- Many families in both the North and the South were divided by the war, and many lost members in battle, particularly in the South.

TEST YOURSELF

These questions will help you discover what you have learned from this book.
Check the pages listed in the answers below.

1. **In the movie *Gone With the Wind*, what does the Southern belle Scarlett O'Hara use to make a dress?**

2. **How tall were most buildings in Northern cities?**

3. **How was a black person in the South punished for seeming rude or disrespectful to a white person?**

4. **Why did some slave owners encourage slaves to have families?**

5. **What substitutes did people in the South use to replace coffee?**

6. **What proportion of Southern men served in the Confederate army?**

7. **What were the relative populations of the North and the South at the start of the war?**

8. **What invention by Gail Borden improved the diet of Union soldiers?**

9. **Why did Southern farmers run short of agricultural tools?**

10. **How could wealthy Northerners avoid the draft?**

ANSWERS

1. Living room drapes (see page 8). 2. Four storys (see page 11). 3. By being beaten or arrested (see page 13). 4. As a way to increase the number of slaves (see page 17). 5. Corn and cotton (see page 20). 6. Three out of every four (see page 23). 7. 22 million in the North and about 9 million in the South (see page 27). 8. Condensed milk (see page 34). 9. The government wanted workshops to make weapons, not tools (see page 35). 10. By paying an exemption fee or hiring a substitute to fight in his place (see page 42).

GLOSSARY

abolition The ending of slavery; supporters of abolition were known as abolitionists

blockade Measures aimed at preventing trade by using ships to intercept vessels heading toward port

Confederacy A league of members united by a common purpose; the word was used to describe the Southern side in the Civil War

conscription The compulsory enrollment of able-bodied people into the armed forces

crinoline A popular style of dress that used a hooped frame to create a bell-like skirt shape

draft Another word for conscription

federal A word referring to the U.S. government in Washington, D.C.

garrison A group of soldiers who occupy a military post

hoard To keep something stored up and hidden away

inflation A steady rise in prices often caused when money loses its value

Lost Cause A popular view of the war in the South that argued that the North had destroyed an ideal society in the South

lynch For a mob to kill someone without any legal authority

militia Part of a country's army made up of citizens who are called on to serve in times of emergency

morale The spirit of feeling of an individual or group of people about whether things will go or are going well or badly

plantation A large-scale agricultural estate; in the South, plantations were used to grow crops such as sugar, tobacco, cotton, and rice

planter Someone who owns a plantation

sanitary association A type of charitable organization that raised money to improve conditions for soldiers in camp

sutler A civilian trader who supplied food to an army post

Union The United States of America; the word described the Northern side in the Civil War

FURTHER READING

BOOKS

Baxter, Roberta. *The Southern Home Front of the Civil War* (Why We Fought: The Civil War). Heinemann Raintree, 2011.

Damon, Duane. *Growing up in the Civil War, 1861–1865* (Our America). Lerner Publications, 2003.

Davis, William C. *Civil War Cookbook*. Courage Books, 2003.

Furbee, Mary Rodd. *Outrageous Women of Civil War Times*. John Wiley & Sons, 2003.

Kreiser, Lawrence A. and Browne, Ray B. *Voices of Civil War America: Contemporary Accounts of Daily Life* (Voices of an Era). Greenwood, 2011.

Mattern, Joanne. *The Big Book of the Civil War: Fascinating Facts about the Civil War*. Courage Books, 2007.

Osborne, Mary Pope. *Civil War on Sunday* (Magic Tree House). Random House, 2000.

Schomp, Virginia. *The Civil War* (Letters from the Homefront). Benchmark Books, 2002.

Stanchak, John E. *Eyewitness Civil War*. Dorling Kindersley, 2000.

Underwood, Josie. *Josie Underwood's Civil War Diary*. The University Press of Kentucky, 2009.

Varhola, Michael J. *Everyday Life During the Civil War*. Writer's Digest Books, 1999.

Varhola, Michael J. *Life in Civil War America*. Family Tree Books, 2011.

Volo, Dorothy Denneen, and Volo, James M. *Daily Life in Civil War America* (Daily Life Through History). Greenwood Press, 2009.

WEBSITES

www.civilwar.com
Comprehensive privately run, moderated site on the Civil War

www.civil-war.net
Collection of images, written sources, and other material about the Civil War

www.historyplace.com/civilwar
The History Place Civil War timeline

www.pbs.org/civilwar
PBS site supporting the Ken Burns film *The Civil War*

www.civilwar.si.edu
The Smithsonian Institution's Civil War collections, with essays, images, and other primary sources

INDEX